THE HOLY LAND

THE UNIVERSIT
WINCHES

MAURICE RIORDAN

The Holy Land

——

faber and faber

First published in 2007
by Faber and Faber Limited
3 Queen Square London WC1N 3AU

Typeset by Faber and Faber Limited
Printed in England by T. J. International Ltd, Padstow, Cornwall

A CIP record for this book
is available from the British Library

ISBN 978–0–571–23464–6
0–571–23464–X

2 4 6 8 10 9 7 5 3 1

i.m. Martin Riordan (1899–1981)

Acknowledgements

Thanks are due to *Chimera*, *Irish Times*, *Magma*, *Ploughshares* (U.S.), *Poetry London*, *Poetry Review*, *New Irish Poetry*, ed. Selina Guinness (Bloodaxe, 2004) and *Tall-lighthouse Review*, where some of these poems have appeared. 'The January Birds' was commissioned for *Wild Reckoning* (Calouste Gulbenkian Foundation, 2004).

I am grateful to the Society of Authors for a Travelling Scholarship; to An Chomhairle Ealaíon/The Arts Council, Ireland, for a travel bursary; and to the Arts Council England for a grant that enabled me to finish this book.

My thanks, too, to Kathryn Maris, Deryn Rees-Jones and Paul Keegan.

Contents

THE HOLY LAND

quand' io dismento nostra vanitate,
trattando l'ombre come cosa salda
Purgatorio, XXI

Mansion Polish

It was from the polish factory in Glanmire
the rain barrels came, one for each corner of the house.
And several more that were cut, hack-sawed lengthwise,
to make troughs for cattle. A few stood round the yard
gathering odds and ends, horseshoes, plough socks,
fallen slates. A hen made a nest in one.

The factory was tucked into the wood behind the village,
the name in iron letters arching the gate.
What was that name? Repeating itself on the tins
of floor-, furniture-, shoe- and harness-polish, which were
    ranged
on a shelf in the pantry, tins my mother used
when empty to hold buttons, pins, pennies . . .
One of them went with me half my life – to France,
to Spain, Canada – because it kept, camouflaged by the coins
and sewing kits, a fateful little love note.

Cattle troughs don't last but the rain barrels . . . I can see
my mother scoop a bucketful from one
to scour the paths. And wet nights I woke,
then slept again to the slap and splash of water
overflowing outside the bedroom window.
In the morning our shoes were paired on newspaper
for the walk to Mass or school. Sometimes
each room gleamed with that interior shine
which may be more vital to the soul than sunlight is.
What was the name? You could see it from the road,
hanging on for years after the factory closed.
I must have driven past a thousand times.

I'm still in my dressing gown, the Sunday papers spread
on the carpet, the sun through the patio doors.
Upstairs there's the ping of a computer game,
a guitar being tuned, the bath is running . . .
The barrels disappeared, a slow burn in the open air.
But the box must be somewhere, in an attic
or on top of someone's wardrobe. It wouldn't
mean much – the name, or the initial on the note.
What was the name? Then it comes to me.
The name on the box. Or was it the box itself?
Just for a moment, giving me the name.

The Holy Land

Father Burns has given us Basil, his greyhound pup,
while he's away himself to the Holy Land.
Basil's track name is Goldfinger.
We believe he's the fastest hound in Christendom.

When he runs round the house his nose appears
at one gable before his tail is gone at the other,
but when we take him to Buttevant for trial
he freezes at the sound of the electric hare.

Although she's loth to vilify a beast
on whom the priest has pinned his hopes,
I hear my mother say under her breath
The little bastard, when he roots up the lily bed.

Basil still streaks around the house
now Father Burns is home and has projected
the holy sights onto Smarts' loft wall: mosaics
and basilicas; Gethsemane, the Mount of Olives.

Then the minibus north through Judea
and Galilee – to Capernaum, Cana,
the water on which He walked, Nazareth
where He was a boy. There too is a basilica.

The Red Sea

for Margaret

When we go to the house together for the last time,
they've taken the floor-coverings up in the kitchen.
I see what was always there but had forgotten:
red cement, with a green diamond at the centre –
where we've been placed with dolls and animals
in the upturned softwood bench, so scored and scribbled
with woodworm you say it's our secret script.
There's a taint in the air of white spirit. Our mother
is on her knees, working towards the open door.
Later she'll reach a plank across the wet paint
and rescue us. But for now the bench is our boat.
I'm gripping a hurley and rowing us in her pursuit.

The Ten Commandments

Our frigate-grey second-hand Ford Anglia
sported a sunshield, a metal peak above the windscreen.
And had a peephole behind the gear handle
through which you could watch the gravel
accelerate, become a shiny brown ribbon
unspooling all the way back to the house.
And when, on the straight into Youghal,
my father finally put his boot to the floor,
the needle shot upright, then swung from side to side.
He laughed, my mother gripped the dashboard,
and the ocean reared above us: a wall of water
more cold fire than water, more the silver flickering
on Smarts' whitewashed wall than the wall itself –
in which we could see the Pharaoh's soldiers
still struggling with their chariots and spears.

The Statue

As a child, as little more than an infant
still learning numbers and words, I went
to sleep after praying for uncles and aunts,
for the living and the dead, with one hand
in my mother's hand through the bars of the cot,
while I held in the other a bronze statuette
of Mary given to me by my godmother,

Sister Rose Teresa, to whom my mother
at the kitchen table wrote *Dear Rita*,
in letters she sent across the ocean
– having copied into them my prayer
for the nuns, which she said they'd treasure,
since *a small boy's words fly to Heaven*
and by the angels there are heard.

So the night Sister Rose was discovered
in the convent bath, we subtracted her
from the living and added her to the dead,
my mother and I, before we prayed,
her hand in one hand, while in the other
I held Mary the Mother of God,
the statue given me by my godmother.

The Parlour

Keegans' land bordered on ours,
though they lived in Carrigtwohill
in a house with a horse's head
sticking out of their front wall.

His four strong legs occupied
the parlour and his tail hung
too close to the fire, my father said –
until the day I followed him in

to find chairs, the table set,
and covering the place
where the head had been severed
was a picture of Pope Pius.

Anniversary

Twenty-three years my father has ripened in death.
Tonight he will come to me as the young bride
who shyly lifts the counterpane from the dream,
lifts the light cloth and fits himself to my side.

Silenus

Her dinner call failed and we went looking –
in out-buildings, along the ditches and the drains.
An unnamed fear stilled the hedges
and the fields were suddenly close and listening.
But we found him safe and sound
asleep beside the stream, his head
propped on a bag of nitrogen,
his Wellington boots under the alders.
When he blinked awake and offered us
that sheepish grin, I guessed
he'd just folded away the woodnotes
and hidden the pipe in his dungarees.

The Idylls

Once upon a time this must have been the Field of Blue Sage.
My goats remember the taste of the grass on the traffic island.
Italo Calvino, *Invisible Cities*

1

One day the men were repairing the fence by the stream in
the Bawn. Moss drove in the stakes with the sledge, while my
father followed with Dan-Jo unwinding the barbed wire and
stapling it loosely to the timber. Then the strands were pulled
taut by the three men and made secure.

'We haven't seen or heard a soul all day,' my father
remarked. 'Not even a tramp or the youngsters from school.'

'Everyone goes round by the road nowadays,' said Dan-Jo.

'And there's no work in the fields any more. No beet to
thin. No sheep to count. No hay to turn and cock and wind.'

'Once you'd have seen twenty men and women in a field at
harvest time.'

'Do you remember the pony races, Moss?'

'I do. The water jump was there by the alders and then the
last jump was into Dillon's Field. The finishing post was by
where the pylon is today.'

'The field black with people.'

'You'd see folk in the fields,' my father continued, 'what-
ever job you were at. Sometimes you'd meet a total stranger
and they'd stop to talk.'

'I drove a pick-up through Manitoba,' Jo said, 'and neither
man nor animal did I see for three days.'

'In the forestry,' Moss said, 'you'd be on your own a lot of
the time. Though you'd hear an axe or a saw from the next
section and you'd be glad of that.'

2

Another day when they were sitting on the headland in the Small Fields, the men discussed the changes they had seen and a debate arose about what was the greatest change had happened in their lifetime.

'What do you think?' My father asked Dan-Jo.

'The steam tractor was a great change,' the trucker answered. 'And then the motor car. But the greatest of all to my mind was the cutter-and-binder.'

'That was a great change,' my father said. 'And you, Alf, what would you say?'

'When the dam was built at Ardnacrusha it flooded farm-land in seven parishes,' said the Gully.

'Yes, that was a great and a terrible change,' my father agreed. 'Moss, you've seen more than any of us. What's your opinion?'

'Women's fashion,' the forester replied. 'Girls these days in next to nothing at Mass.'

My father nodded, 'That too is a great change.' And the rest chipped in and everyone had a different opinion about what was the greatest change in their lifetime: television, the creamery, penicillin, Shannon airport, the price of stout, false teeth, tourists, the electric fence, plastic bags, weedkiller.

'There are a lot of changes,' my father said.

Moss turned to him, 'Tell us, Martin, what you think.'

My father fished in his inside pocket and took out a small framed photo of a woman in a wide hat and veil, smiling happily.

'That,' he said, 'is my mother on her honeymoon.'

3

'The fish are all but gone.'

The men had spent the day under the sun drawing in hay from the Kiln Field. In the cool of evening they led Billy and Jack and Nance, the mare, down to the pond. They stood in the mud dousing the horses and each other with the sweet-tin.

'The trout used to come upstream this far,' my father continued. 'You'd spot them darting away when bringing the cows to water. Now you'd never find one further up than the Glens.'

'And you never hear the bittern anymore,' said Dan-Jo.

'Or see a newt,' added Moss.

'Hardly ever an otter.'

'Even lady wagtails are a rare sight.'

'There's still no shortage of pigeons and crows,' Davey Divine said.

'It must be artificial fertilizer.'

'Maybe it's the chemicals in the spray.'

'It could be,' Moss said, 'that the plantation of Stretch's Mountain upset the water table.'

'It's a curse whatever it is,' said my father. 'A blight. One time this place could provision an army. I tell you in September the mushroom pickers from the city were out in the Kiln Field from dawn till dinner. There were snipe in the Bogs in winter, and teal and widgeon. The rushes were alive with frogs and eels. There were woodlarks, yellowhammers, fieldfares, flocks of lapwing and golden plover, starlings thicker than storm clouds. You'd see a kingfisher first thing on a misty morning. The heron in the stream as still as a post.'

'And a hawk high overhead. Or an eagle.'

4

'Once, a warm hazy evening in the fall of the year, a red
deer appeared at the end of the Long Field. It was a buck
with a fine rack of antlers. It must have come from Curragh
Wood, though how it got to be there is anybody's guess.
There was no barbed wire then on the ditches and gaps were
often left open. It stopped to browse with the herd. It moved
among the cows lifting its bony great head. But they took lit-
tle notice. And then it made its way up the lane and into the
yard. The dogs growled and by now everyone had stepped
out of the house to have a look. A couple of the lads had
guns. But the deer hopped over the Haggard wall, and it con-
tinued on up through the Hill Fields. It crossed the road and
vanished into Stretch's Mountain.'

'Did no one think to shoot it?' asked Davey Divine.

'No one shot it,' my father said.

5

'That's the Hunter rising behind Curragh Wood,' said my father.

It was a biting cold night in January. We were in the Hill Fields with Goldfinger, the priest's greyhound. Davey Divine was holding a headlamp and using it for a torch. He had unscrewed it from the tractor earlier along with the battery. Dan-Jo was carrying the battery.

'Otherwise known as Orion. Although he was a Greek and never an Irishman.'

The plan was to dazzle a hare and get the hound to chase it. It would give him a taste for coursing. All we could find were rabbits and Goldfinger was shivering from the cold. Or else he was afraid of the dark. Or of the light.

'That's his belt, those three stars at a diagonal.'

Davey raked the light over the uneven ground until he located a rabbit grazing. The rabbit looked up, his eyes caught in the beam.

'Go on, Goldfinger, get him!'

'And the bright star at his heel is Canis Major.'

'But it's only a rabbit, Davey.'

'Let him off the leash, Jo.'

Dan-Jo unleashed the hound and gave him a push. 'Go on, Goldfinger, get him now!'

'It's as if he's crouched above the wood ready to spring.'

The rabbit started to run.

6

The Bo'son arrived one harvest evening. He walked in the Passage while the men were at their supper and took a berth in the loft without a word. No one enquired who he was, or asked if he'd run away from home, or from a Home, if he was an army deserter or fresh out of jail. But you could see he wasn't accustomed to farm work. When my father told him to sharpen the scythe, he sawed the whetstone back and forth across the edge.

'It's not like you're playing a fiddle with the bow, son!' said Moss, taking the scythe to show him how it should be done. That's how he came to be known as the Bo'son.

One day the Harvester didn't show up. It was a fine morning. The dew had dried from the ground by breakfast and the ears of barley were crackling in the heat. But the silver Claes combine stood idle in the middle of Higgs's Field. The men replaced damaged sections on the blade. They climbed onto the platform and folded clean sacks for the chutes. They cut lengths of binder twine for tying the sacks when they were filled. The Bo'son had gone underneath the combine and was greasing the nipples.

It was mid-morning. The Harvester still hadn't showed. The men patted the dogs and lazed about. The Bo'son was sitting up on the driver's seat. Suddenly the machine started into life. The engine revved and belts and flywheels began to turn. The worm rotated. Then the combine set off bouncing across the stubble ground. But 'Son steered it round to face the uncut field. He lowered the blade into the standing barley.

The machine rumbled and shuddered from end to end. It coughed diesel smoke into the air and chaff flew from its tail.

'Don't just stand there gawping!' my father roared. The men scrambled to grab hold of the platform ladder, while the grain from the open chutes rained about their heads.

7

'We're more or less standing on the water table.'

The men were in the Bog waist deep in muddy ground. They were cutting a drain from the pond to the stream. The hope was to free up land for pasture and my father was following instructions from the Department Engineer. 'You could say the water is meant to run from head to toe, while the people go east and west across it.'

'In former times,' he explained, 'an old road came through the farm and exited via Keegan's Passage onto the Pound Road, then away towards the city. By day and even at night there was a traffic of carts and people driving animals, of men on horseback, tinkers, hawkers, constabulary. All sorts, who might stop at the pump for talk and refreshment.'

'Were there no rogues and thieves in those days?' asked Davey Divine.

'A duck or a rabbit might go missing but never anything of value.'

'Though the road's no longer in use there are still those who know,' said Moss. 'Tramps and trappers and suchlike. They hold onto things longer than most. And they remember the paths and where the stepping stones are.'

'So that's how you'd find Carney the Knacker or Snook Buckley asleep beside you on a cold morning.'

'If it's beside you he'd be, 'Son. But you were saying about the water?'

'Well, in Alice Warren's time they diverted the water to create a lake.'

'What was a lake for?'

'God only knows,' Moss said. 'The Warrens were English.'

'Pleasure, I suppose.'

My father traced the course of the water along the south side of the Paddock. There it looped around like a moat outside the high stone walls of the yard. He pointed to the hollow where the geese were grazing below the Lane Gate. 'You can see the brooklime's taken over and it's a softer green. That's where it was.'

By now the men had stopped their work. They had climbed out of the drain and were looking back across the rushes and furze bushes towards the farm yard, picturing what it must have been like.

'A lake,' said Davey at last. 'A pleasure lake.'

8

'Nowhere else but in Rome had he tasted water the like of it. Monsignor Ronan's very words.' My father was walking the wheat in the Building Field with the new Government Inspector. His face was flushed red. The grain had contracted rust and the question was whether to harvest it for feed or plough it back into the soil.

The men stood side by side under the shade of the poplars and awaited the outcome.

'I can't see him get his way on this occasion,' said Moss.

'She's got a fine pair of headlamps though,' said Davey. 'Like a Volvo.'

'Shhh . . . She'll hear you.'

'He's at the end of his rope.'

'Or a new Citroën –'

''Son, hurry to the spout,' my father called out just then, 'and fetch the lady refreshment.' He turned once more to the new Government Inspector. The wheat sloped away towards the lower Glens. It shimmered and darkened like a cloth of gold as the *sidhe gaoithe* criss-crossed the land. Snatches of conversation came to us on the air over the crackling heads of grain. 'Fungus . . . ruin . . . better to burn . . . all very well . . . ha . . .' The two of them turned about and about again.

When they returned to the shade, 'Son handed her the sweet-tin brimming with the icy liquid.

'You should try it with a drop of Paddy,' said my father, taking the half-pint from his inside pocket.

'Thank you but I won't, Mister O'Reardon. No alcohol you know on duty.' She dipped her fingers in the water and tasted it. Then she leaned her head back and drank slowly from the tin.

'As I was saying, the new Citroën –'

'Christ, Davey!'

My father stood apart on the headland, his eyes lowered to the ground.

'– has hydraulic suspension.'

9

It was only mud, my father said. Nothing but muck and mud.

He had stormed into the house and was threatening to sell the farm. He was putting it under the hammer, he said. It no longer afforded any sort of life. And who had he to pass it on to? No one knew where the bounds' ditch was. No one but himself and maybe the dog. They mightn't credit him but the For Sale sign was going up. He'd met a man in Fermoy who wanted to buy the whole shagging lot for a golf course.

My mother said why didn't he sell to him then, and to shut up about it.

But Moss said 'twas only the whiskey talking. In the morning he'd have forgotten about it. And they would be out in the fields the same as always.

10

'When we first got the electric fence we went short of wire.'

The fence ran along the boundary with Keegan's and it was intended to stop the cattle from trespassing on his sugar beet. The battery was located on the west bank of the stream for safe keeping. But another few yards of wire were needed to span the water and complete the circuit. It looked like it would have to wait.

'You could try this,' said the Bo'son handing my father a length of plastic pipe. It was a piece left over from when the water was taken up to the new dwelling house.

'You're going to have to show us.'

The Bo'son laid the pipe along the bed of the stream and told Moss to put some stones on top to keep it under water. He blocked up the two ends of the pipe with putty. Then he pushed the fence wire in at one end and the battery connection in at the other.

'Put your hand on the fence,' my father told Dan-Jo.

Ha, he leapt two feet in the air and swore like Beelzebub.

'It works, but how?'

'It's what they did on the Indian Telegraph,' said the Bo'son. 'Except instead of pipe they used a two-and-a-half mile stretch of the Hooghly River.'

'It must be a corruption of some sort,' said Donal.

Our cousin had come to help with the potatoes during the Easter holidays. We were working along the drills in pairs, slicing the seed in halves and planting them a foot apart in the Pawk Re-og. 'The only field on the farm with an Irish name,' my father had said.

'Danny Boy, you being the next best thing to a professor, you'll be able to tell us what it means.'

'From *páirc* of course. And *réidh*, meaning smooth. The Smooth Field?'

'The Rough Field, more like,' said Davey Divine, straightening his back.

'*Réidh* could also mean any place flat. Open untilled land. A heath or a moor. What do you think, Uncle Martin?'

'I think we might be wasting your time with the spuds.'

'Isn't it peculiar, though, the only native name among the fields.'

'I don't have a word of Irish,' my father said, 'but I'll tell you what it is. It's a burial ground.'

'*Reilig.*'

'You mean like Han's Bed?'

'No. This place was used to bury people during the famine.'

'It's hard to believe we're in a graveyard,' said Davey looking around. 'Without headstones.'

'This was once English land,' my father said. 'You can tell from the masonry. Even the culvert there carrying water to the pond has a keystone. And look at the height of the Paddock walls, what's standing of them. That was where they kept deer.'

'Tame deer,' said cousin Donal. 'Red meat.'

'This is not like other fields,' said 'Son. 'The trees are remote.'

'The Gully will bring Éil Dade later on here. For a court in the long grass.'

'Not as long as your nose, Divine.'

'The long and short of it is Colonel Warren owned all this,' my father continued. 'And John Keegan's across the ditch. The people came down the Leamlara Road from Bartlemy and Carrignavar and Killavullen. From the hills to the north. They were going to the boat in Queenstown, living off the wayside. A number of those who died were given burial in this field.'

12

As it happened, my uncle Tom the Buck was home the morning John Keegan's bull appeared on the bounds' ditch. The men were at their breakfast when they heard his bellow. They grabbed pitchforks and rushed out the West Gate to confront him. By now the bull had broken through the electric fence and was sauntering across the Bog, making for the heifers in the Big Lawn. Uncle Tom had brought along his rifle.

'I can bring him down from here.'

'No,' said my father. He told Jo to start the tractor. He perched on the drawbar and the two of them set out over the Bog. The bull had broken into a run but the soft ground was holding him back. They headed him off when he cleared the new drain and turned him into the pond.

He stood knee-deep in the ooze, snorting through his nose ring, his pink pizzle plain for all to see.

'The cheeky fucker,' said Davey aiming the pitchfork at his eyes. But the bull charged, knocking Davey over, and made a break for the Paddock. The tractor kept chase. Round and round the enclosure they went. At last the bull stood his ground, his ribcage heaving.

A crowd had gathered behind the West Gate.

My father got hold of the nose ring. 'We'll get him into the cattle crush.' He shoved the prongs of the pitchfork into his dewlap and at the same time pulled hard on the ring. Blood dropped from the nostrils and the dark eyes milked over. My father walked backwards one foot at a time, wheeling the bull until he had brought him to the mouth of the crush. He nodded to the men. Moss dawked the bull in the bollocks with his pike, and as he sprang my father stepped to the side.

The bull went straight in. The bars shook but they held. Someone slammed the gate on his hindquarters and my father shot one bolt under his neck, another under his belly.

A cheer went up.

'You can lower that now,' my father said to the Buck.

My uncle swivelled on his heel, dropped to one knee, and fired in the direction of the disused shed. The rusted heavy padlock on the door pinged. Once, twice.

13

'It reminds you, Moss.'

It was nightfall late August. The men were in the Pound smoking after supper. The air was heavy and a haze had dimmed the stars and darkened the tops of the Scots pines. The fog horn boomed softly from the estuary. But you could see the lights from Whitegate oil refinery above the brim of Curragh Wood.

'The gunboat left the city at eight.'

'The *Asgard*, was it? Or the *Grainne*?'

'We heard the salute as she set off from Albert Quay.'

'The Big Fellow,' Davey remarked.

'They say Emmet Dalton never once left his side.'

'His aide-de-camp.'

'Not that we were altogether of his opinion.'

'We thought we heard the banshee that night. Though it turned out next day it was young Mrs Sliney crying and wandering the road in her nightdress. Paddy had given her a slap and locked her outside.'

'As he was wont to do.'

'The people came out from the houses.'

'Flares went up and the hooter sounded as she came down the fairway.'

'Past Blackrock.'

'Rushbrooke, Ringaskiddy.'

'Cobh.'

'Queenstown, as it was still called.'

'Haulbowline, Spike Island, Roche's Point.'

'Then out to sea.'

14

'There were the Driscoll brothers of Mownbawn.
One of the Connells, and a cousin of theirs?'
'Corcoran.' 'The jockey from Peafield, Shea.'
'A bantamweight, they said was shot at dawn.'
'I can't name them all, but more than in our own
War of Independence.' 'Or the Troubles after.'
'Young Standish Barry, part-reared across the water.'
'Who rose to be a captain, the last of a line.'
'He came out alive.' 'Though never right in his mind.'
'Mill workers, itinerant labourers, sons of cottiers,
boys who couldn't do a sum or write their name,
who'd never left Lisgoold' – 'were shipped for Flanders.'
'They died, Moss, on the Somme and on the Marne.'
'They died for the same wet and muck, Martin.'

15

'It's a mystery where he's gone.'

It was the morning after dragging the river. Young Hyland had been fishing for trout with onion bags and had drowned in a pool. The men had worked through the night by the light of storm lamps. But the body hadn't been recovered. They had come home to see to the cows and were drinking whiskey in the Old House while their clothes dried before the fire.

'It's a mystery how it happened in the first place.'

'They said when he went under he never came to the surface again, though they thought they heard him call three times.'

'His foot must have been caught by a root.'

'Maybe he was pulled down by a current or a whirlpool.'

'It's not as if this is the Blackwater.'

'They say it takes three lives a year,' said Davey Divine. 'The bodies often turn up miles downstream or are washed in from the ocean months after.'

'I wouldn't want to be the one to come upon them then,' said Moss.

'Still they say it's not the worst way to go.'

'I always drown the kittens and pups,' said Jo. 'Better that than stringing them from the clothes-line.'

'Or feeding them to the sow, like the Gully does.'

'I think it must be frightening to die under the water.'

'Why do you think that, 'Son?'

'Because how would you be able to say the Act of Contrition?'

The men laughed. 'Maybe you should keep away from those Coakley sisters.'

My father said, 'I think, 'Son, it would be enough to repeat the words in your head.'

16

hoor-u-hoor-u-oo-u

The men had come home flaming from Pigeon Hill races. On clear evenings the walls of the old Deer Park gave back an echo. It was a starlit night at the end of May and we were woken in the small hours by the rumpus from the Haggard. Davey and 'Son were giving it a go.

Gold-finger!

ole-in-gerr-err-rr

'They've frightened the little creatures.'

'They'll wake the whole country.'

'They'll wake the dead, woman.'

My father had appeared in his nightshirt.

He took the shotgun down from the hall stand and loaded both its barrels, then flung wide the back door. The night air blew in.

O'Reardon!

o-airdin-airin-air-nn

Han the Heifer!

an-deffer-effer-eff-rr

'I'll give them . . . what for.'

'Martin, no! Let them be. They're only play-acting.' She smiled at him. 'Besides they might set the dog on you.'

We could see over his shoulder the moon in swift flight above the tops of the Scots pines. The cold draught blew the loose shirt against his knees and chest. He pulled the door to again. 'I suppose they'll wear out.'

He withdrew the cartridges and replaced the gun on the hall stand. Goldfinger had begun to howl and Keegan's collie replied, faintly from the distance. 'The poor motherless bastards,' my father said, turning for the bedroom. 'They'll have heads on them tomorrow morning.'

17

'Does the apple let go of the tree – or does the tree give it a nudge?'

We were in the Orchard gathering the windfalls before school. St Martin's Summer, the frost turning to dew or the dew already becoming frost. Unbroken spider webs joined branch to branch and tree to tree, the Bramleys to the Pippins, the Golden Russets to the Blenheim Oranges, the crab apple to our ancient Calville Blank Diver.

So: does the fledgling take wing or do the parent birds push it from the nest? Does the soul abandon the body or the body with its last strength send it on its way? Does the Father beget the Son, or is the Son one with the Father? Do the living replace the dead or do the dead souls hinder the living? Does the hand cast the stone? Or does the stone wriggle from the hand? We were in the Orchard gathering windfalls. We filled our caps and aprons, though there was no wind that year.

18

Davey, the Bo'son and myself were with my father topping beet in Buckleys' Field. We pulled the muddy tubers out of the ground, trimmed the roots with the blade, then sliced off the green heads and tossed the finished beet into a wicker barrow. A north-east wind was blowing down from the Galtees and sending black squalls of rain and sleet across the open country.

The light faded and my father proposed a halt. We stood together in the lee of the beech.

'It's no beauty spot, the dead end of October.'

'On fine nights,' my father said, 'Moss used to lie out on the old lime kiln under the stars. One time he nodded off and he damn near finished up in the kiln.'

The Bo'son said he liked lying on the Haggard wall after supper and listening to the wind in the pines. 'The air in the Haggard is soft, almost like a woman's breath.'

'You can't ever have been in the van with Éil Dade then.'

But Davey said he preferred company, even if it was only someone to argue with. Oftentimes now he sat by the well and played a tune on the whistle. 'Just to myself and the hound.'

'And what about you, Boss, who knows every rood of the land. What is your favourite haunt?'

My father said it was Colman's Glen. 'Where the sloe bush straddles the stream. And there's never a soul, only the birds. That's the place I'll be spending my holidays.'

Mediums

Acts 2:13

§

He drank only *mejums* on his outings
to marts, funerals, race meetings.
After a few he'd break into song.
A few more and he spoke in tongues.

§

My father hops across nimble as a piebald pony,
then lifts the single strand of electrified wire
for myself to follow after.

We're on a mission to retrieve a heifer
out of Keegan's sugar beet, but have detoured
by way of Lesseps and the Parc Guell.

A white-faced Hereford, who's made daylight
of Keegan's ditch to find somewhat more to her liking
than our green-and-gold strip

of furze and ragwort, more in keeping with her forebears,
maybe, on the Welsh marches – or has she smelled
the strawberry fields of Tibidabo?

My father lifts the strand of rusted wire,
careful it won't snag on the T-shirt
I bought this morning on the Ramblas.

Even so, it shows all the wilfulness
of the pup Goldfinger on a leash,
or a mountain hare drawn by Miro,

and whips back to catch the *e* of *libre*
smack in the eye, drawing blood
from the apostolic face of Che Guevara.

§

'I heard of this fellow out in Africa.'
With one hand he upends a ewe, with the other
settles her between his knees. 'A doctor.
Women came to him, young married girls
from the forests and mountain villages
who suffered a complaint of the bladder,
a leak brought about when they gave birth.
They smelled. They were sent away in shame,
banished to an outhouse from their homes.'
He pares the hoof with the open blade.
'But this chap had a remedy, a cure.
He'd snip some flesh from . . . another place
and patch them like you'd mend a puncture.
Women flocked to him from all over.
They walked Swedish miles or hitched by jeep.
A girl sat on that country's border
one whole year to beg the bus fare.'
He cleans the cleft and rubs the bluestone in.
The ewe regains her legs and steps,
a little gingerly. 'That should do the trick.
And what I remember was when they healed,
his wife gave them each a cotton frock
of poppy red or green or stripy yellow.
A new dress to go home in – nothing lavish,
but something that had a splash of colour.'

§

I didn't get where I am by wearing underpants decorated with
    Beethoven.
Or the Red Flag, my father said. Or even the Turin Shroud.
I didn't get where I am on the Orient Express.
I didn't get where I am by taking night-classes in Chinese.
I didn't get where I am by taking my eye off the ball,
by putting the cart in front of the horse or by turning the other
    cheek.
I didn't get where I am eating figs and olives and gherkins.
I didn't get where I am in Malibu.
I didn't get where I am with yoga, feng shui, cranial massage or
    acupuncture.
I didn't get where I am in wigwams.
I didn't get where I am on the snows of Kilimanjaro, or on
    a pilgrimage to Saint James of Compostela.
Nor did I get where I am because your mother prayed every
    night to Saint Jude.
I didn't get where I am beholden to any man.
I didn't get where I am at the Fleadh Ceoil.
I didn't get where I am at the Munster Final.
I didn't get where I am at the Sorbonne.
I didn't get where I am in pub, club or club-house.
I didn't get where I am on the camel's back.
Nor did I get where I am in the Order of the Golden Dawn,
    or by joining the Royal Society for the Protection of Bullshit.
I didn't get where I am by thinking it would all sound a lot better
in Italian, that you could put a tune to it
if only it were in Aramaic or Mandarin Chinese.
No, that's not how I got where I am.

[40]

§

[he says a poem learnt at his mother's knee]

John Northridge was a farmer snug who lived in lush Kildare.
One day a tramp came by and said, 'I'm of the Burren, Clare.
I'm hungry and I'm thirsty and my name is Dan Maguire,
And would it please your honour, Sir, to take me on for hire.'
The farmer looked him up and down and finally he said,
'I'll give you bite and sup if you weed that cabbage bed.'
Dan started off with ready will – but only worth a while,
For all at once he stopped his toil and smiled a cunning smile.
'Aye, Mister Northridge, Sir!' The farmer was at hand.
'I'm sure you've heard it said an empty sack can't stand?'
'You're right, my Christian boy! So just you step inside.'
And a truly splendid feast to Dan he quick supplied.
Dan ate and drank with eager zest, but when the plate
Was polished off, he found the door and bolted for the gate.
'Come back,' the irate farmer called, 'and to your work
    attend!'
'Aye, Green Guts Northridge, Sir,' said Dan, 'a full sack
    won't bend.'

§

With one hand he steadies a bull calf,
places the clamps then snaps them shut.
'Recall how you followed from field to field,
tagging along like a dog at my heel.
Except you'd get more out of the dog.
Not one word from you – the day I said
I'll do myself in, AS MANY HAVE DONE ROUND HERE.'
The calf regains his legs – a shiver, a moo,
then trots off to rejoin the herd.
'I had to say *let's go count the sheep*.
I had to break stride to reassure you,
I had to say *you count their legs,*
and I'll divide what you get by four.
Let's face it, you turned for home then,
soon as you'd gained the upper hand.
I could ask what you think about that now.'

§

'I love it in Keegan's Passage this time of year
with the white and the pink-and-white
Christmas trees on the chestnut trees.'
He whistles a rusty old tune.

I love to wander down the old boreen
When the hawthorn blossoms are in bloom
Or to sit by the gate on the old mossy sate
A-whisperin' to Kate Muldoon

§

He breaks the ice and frees the ballcock,
his eye at some point in Keegan's beet.
'I don't detect a woman in your life.
Not one other life longside your own.
To whom you cleave?' With the penknife
he turns the valve. The pipe coughs out
rust and air, then runs. 'It's all the weight
of Stretch's Mountain pressing on
the water table.' The cattle trough,
a rain barrel sawed along its length,
fills to overflowing. 'You're past your prime
and have avoided this. I can only wish
a happier course to your decline.'

§

[he begins with a line by Sandy Lyle]

There's more to life than hitting a golf ball
and more to life than this bitch the farming life,
more to it than lying in a hammock at Bill Duffy's farm.
There's more to life than wasting one's life,
though there's more life in wasters than you'd think.
Though it's more thinking what life is like
than it is the thing itself.
For the thing about life is it's crazier and more of it than
    you think.
And the more there is the more we want
and what we want we live to regret,
for what one wants one gets too late or spends too quick.
Getting and regretting we lay waste our powers,
and it is the waste remains and kills.
One could do worse than lay in a hammock all one's life,
and take up late in life the game of golf.

Understorey

§

'A fellow could hide out in here for a season.'
He draws the briars aside and ushers me in
to the understorey. 'See, dry as a public house.'
The sycamore fills with wind, and a flash
reddens the bare ground as the heavens open.
'The day your children are born you'll be due
at one of those tomfool parties, but that night
you'll spend in a room of tubes and bird alarms.
I see you there, a hand through the porthole
of a Perspex cot, holding a child's hand in yours.
You're looking out at traffic on the flyovers.
It makes no sound, you think, and you look back
at the child whose mouth shapes and reshapes
its empty scream: *the sound we never hear*
from the prisons and the slaughter houses,
from the darkened corners of the globe.
We belong in an uncountable world but one
where now by a freak of chance you've gained
a slippery grip – on that same night an airliner
jack-knifes into a mountain of Japan, all lives lost.
Though you'll read how days later an infant
was found in a tree, breathing in its mother's arms.'
The rain pauses. We emerge into Higgs's Field.
Two snipe take off, zigzagging towards the Glens.
'See, all you'd want is a Primus and a coil of wire.'
He clears his throat of phlegm. 'There were other
    things . . .
cross words, music . . . things I couldn't get, or better

left alone – but eight years on you'll recount it all
in a tea-shop on the Welsh borders to someone
half your age whose eyes are pools of rain.
It's May again, and you tell her how the cars
and lorries never ceased on the flyover.
But at some point the traffic of that night
became the traffic of next morning.'

§

A shoal of starlings lifts and skims the bounds
at our approach. Beyond, in the muddy stubble,
plover and lapwing graze between the cows.

They can't see me. He shakes his blackthorn
in anger – or in greeting? *See, they can't see me!*
He laughs. 'It means I'll not live to see them born.'

We've come to the Bottom Glen, where the stream
goes under alder and bog myrtle, then drops
through barbs of rusty furze to Dillon's field.

'This is where the souls of all our line await
their hour of coming hither. And those two
in the crowd – the one so shy she hides her face

in hair and hardly dares to look your way,
and that other with the game leg whose sight
is dimmed but whose gaze is bared to heaven,

his forehead flaming like some young colt's –
they will be yours, your lot. You, once scorched
by their souls' twin-flame, will seek your destiny.

But you'll need courage then to untie your tongue,
strength too in the face of ignominy and insult.
Should you succeed, it will be due to them.

We've come to the end. Look over your shoulder
– but not towards the house – and you'll find
we have erased each field even as we walked.

The way ahead is over water, the way back
through landfill, rubble, roundabouts and raw estates
– Finnsgrove, Meadowvale, Elsinore Heights.

Streets where once were fields like those I tilled,
with foreign makes of car parked up drives
where mares in foal have stood, and men with pikes.

And the Bucks' Gate where the Tans one night stalled
their Crossley Tender – they didn't come within
but swore and relieved themselves against our wall –

you'll find it's bulldozed wide, our old passage
now once more a public right of way for folk
I've not met and have no wish to meet.

I never dealt in life with a man or woman whose name
I didn't know, whose kin I had not followed
or shouldered to their plot of consecrated ground.

But you belong to different times, you who are the age
I was the day you were born. By then I was too old
for all this, and now I've nothing more to give.

Do not flinch. Is not that the outside light come on
in Colman's yard? I should better go. But here,
take my old coat, and this my beaten hat for headgear.'

With that he swung his compact frame about and went,
nearby that stunted bush with its stringy beard of catkin.
His words with birdcalls mingled in the pissing rain.

§

I touch the oily sweat band
and rummage through the old coat.

In an inside pocket is the penknife
I'd bought myself at Carrig races,

the handle worn thin, its blade still keen.
And with it hayseeds, a cartridge, dockets

from Hyde's, the numbers faded;
tuppence, some sloes, a small hole.

The January Birds

The birds in Nunhead Cemetery begin
Before I've flicked a switch, turned on the gas.
There must be some advantage to the light

I tell myself, viewing my slackened chin
Mirrored in the rain-dark window glass,
While from the graveyard's trees, the birds begin.

An image from a dream survives the night,
Some dreck my head refuses to encompass.
There must be some advantage to the light.

You are you I mouth to my shadow skin,
Though you are me, assuming weight and mass –
While from the graveyard's trees, the birds begin:

Thrush, blackbird, finch – then rooks take fright
At a skip-truck and protest, cawing en masse.
There must be some advantage to the light

Or birds would need the gift of second sight
To sing *Another year will come to pass!*
The birds in Nunhead Cemetery begin,
There must be some advantage to the light.

Notes

'Mediums': 'And they began to speak with divers tongues, according as the Holy Ghost gave them to speak . . . And they were all astonished, and wondered, saying one to another: What meaneth this? But others mocking, said: These men are full of new wine.' (Acts 2:4–13). Literally in Aramaic, verse 13 reads: 'Others, however, laughed at them, as they said, "They have been drinking distilled [alcohol] and are drunk."'

mejum (i.e. medium): half-pint of porter.

CJ: character in 1970s sitcom *The Rise and Fall of Reginald Perrin*.

Sandy Lyle: it may have been Greg Norman, or Colin Montgomery.

'The January Birds': thrushes and blackbirds shouldn't be singing in January.